A ROOKIE BIOGRAPHY

ELIZABETH THE FIRST

Queen of England

By Carol Greene

CHILDRENS PRESS®

CHICAGO

This book is for Katie, Peggy, and Molly Thacker.

LIBRARY OF CONGRESS
Library of Congress Cataloging-in-Publication Data

Greene, Carol.
    Elizabeth the First : (Queen of England) / by Carol Greene
       p. cm. — (A Rookie biography)
    Includes index.
    Summary: Describes in simple terms the life of Queen Elizabeth I
of England.
    ISBN 0-516-04214-9
    1. Elizabeth I, Queen of England, 1533-1603—Juvenile literature.
2. Great Britain—Kings and rulers—Biography—Juvenile literature.
3. Great Britain—History—Elizabeth, 1558-1603—Juvenile literatures.
[1. Elizabeth I, Queen of England, 1533-1603—Juvenile literature.
2. Kings, queens, rulers, etc. 3. Great Britain—History—Elizabeth, 1559-
1603.] I. Title. II. Series: Greene, Carol. Rookie biography.
DA355.G75   1990
942.05'5'092—dc20
[B]
[92]   90-2204
                                        CIP
                                        AC

Elizabeth the First
was a real person
and a great queen.
She was born in 1533.
She died in 1603.
Elizabeth ruled England
for almost 45 years.
This is her story.

TABLE OF CONTENTS

Henry the Eighth (left) ruled England from 1509 to 1547. Henry divorced his first wife and married Anne Boleyn, shown below holding hands with Henry. Elizabeth was the daughter of Anne Boleyn and Henry the Eighth.

Chapter 1

The Young Princess

Henry the Eighth,
king of England,
wanted a baby boy.
Henry thought
a boy could be king
after him.
A girl couldn't.

His first wife had a girl.
Henry divorced her.
Now his second wife,
Queen Anne, was going
to have a baby.

"It *must* be a boy,"
said everyone.
But it was another girl,
little Princess Elizabeth.
No one was glad to see her.

Elizabeth and her half sister,
Mary, lived in the country
at Hatfield Palace.
They almost never
saw their parents.
Other people took care of them.

Hatfield was a good place.
It had a park full of deer,
and people were kind.
Elizabeth loved it.

One day, King Henry said
that Queen Anne was bad.
He had her head cut off.
Elizabeth didn't really know
what happened to her mother.
She was only two years old.

Anne Boleyn (left) was
accused of treason and
sent to the Tower of London.
she was found guilty
of treason and
beheaded in 1536 (below).

When Elizabeth was four,
Henry's next wife
had a boy, Edward.
Soon he came to Hatfield
and Elizabeth had
someone new to love.

Before long, Elizabeth began
to study and learn.
A princess must know a lot.
She learned writing, music,
five languages, and religion.
Elizabeth was smart.

She also learned to shoot
with a bow and arrow.
She liked that.
And she learned to sew.
She didn't like that.

**Princess Elizabeth was a good student.
She could speak five different languages.**

When King Henry the
Eighth died in 1547,
the half brother of
Elizabeth (left),
nine-year-old
Prince Edward (below)
was crowned king.
Edward was the only
male child Henry the
Eighth ever had.

Edward the Sixth (1537-1553)
was the son of Jane Seymour,
the third wife of Henry the Eighth.

When Elizabeth
was 13, Henry
died and Edward
became king.
But he was
only nine.
Other people
ruled for him.

R.TAYLOR

Poor Edward was never
very strong or healthy.
He died when he was 15.

Queen Mary was the daughter of Henry the Eighth
and his first wife, Catherine of Aragon.
She was a Catholic and because of her
persecution of the Protestants
she was called "Bloody Mary."

Then Mary became queen
and bad times began
for England and
Princess Elizabeth.

Chapter 2

The Unhappy Queen

Mary was a gloomy
and cruel queen.
People didn't like her.
Even her husband
didn't like her.
He married her to get power.

Mary the First (1516-1558)
became queen of
England in 1553.

But the people liked Elizabeth.
Many thought she would be
a better queen than Mary.
One day, some people
tried to make her queen.

Mary's husband,
Philip the Second
(1527-1598) became
king of Spain in 1556.

Princess Elizabeth was sent to the Tower of London
by her half sister, Queen Mary.

Elizabeth didn't help them
and their plan failed.
But Mary was furious.
She locked Elizabeth up
in the Tower of London.

Elizabeth was afraid.
She had done no wrong.
But what if Mary had
her head cut off anyway?

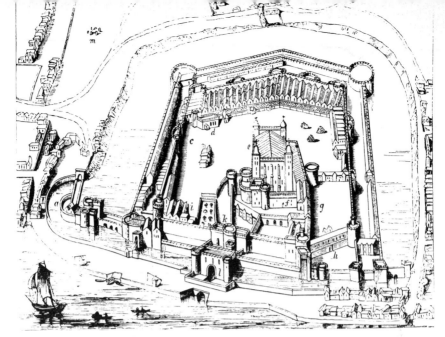

The Tower of London
as it appeared
in 1597. The
features marked
are a. Lion's Tower;
b. Bell Tower;
c. Beauchamp Tower;
d. The Chapel;
e. Keep
     or the White Tower;
f. Jewel-house;
g. Queen's Lodgings;
h. Queens Gallery
     and Garden;
i. Lieutenant's Lodgings;
k. Bloody Tower;
l. St. Thomas's Tower
     (now Traitor's Gate);
m. Place of Execution
     on Tower Hill

But Queen Mary knew that
she must not kill Elizabeth.
Too many people liked her.
so she sent Elizabeth
far away to Woodstock Palace.

After a while, Mary
set Elizabeth free.
But Elizabeth didn't feel safe.
People still liked her best
and Mary knew that.

During the reign of Queen Mary, the poor people of England became poorer.

As the years passed,
life in England
grew worse and worse.
Many people were poor.
Many died of flu.
There was war with France.

Mary had people killed
who did not share
her ideas about religion.
She became known
as "Bloody Mary."

Queen Elizabeth
was crowned in
St. Paul's Cathedral.

Then, when Elizabeth
was 25, Mary died.
Church bells rang joyfully,
because England had
a new queen,
Elizabeth the First.

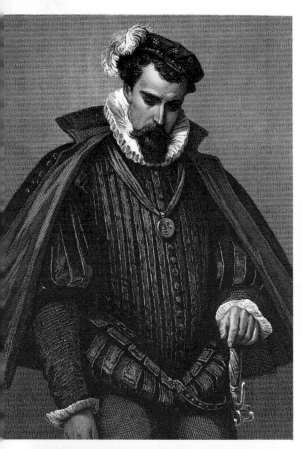

Queen Elizabeth asked
Robert Dudley (top left)
and William Cecil (left)
to help her rule England.

Chapter 3

A Queen's Life

Elizabeth loved being queen.
She wasn't afraid anymore.
She wanted to rule.

As soon as she could,
she tried to stop people
from fighting about religion.
Elizabeth loved peace, too.

A queen must pick
people to help her rule.
William Cecil was
Elizabeth's best helper.
But Robert Dudley
and other people helped her, too.

Many men wanted
to marry Elizabeth.
Some were rulers.
Some were not.
She told them all no.

She liked Dudley a lot.
But she knew he wasn't
the right man to marry.

Then Elizabeth caught smallpox.
She was very sick.

"What if she dies?"
asked everyone.
"She isn't married.
She has no children.
Who will rule after her?"

Queen Elizabeth's court became a meeting place
for musicians, artists, writers, and scholars.

But Elizabeth didn't die
and she didn't get married.
In a way, she felt that
the people she ruled
were her children
and she was their mother.

The people loved her, too.
Poets wrote poems about her.
Musicians wrote music.
Elizabeth liked that.

Of course, she had problems.
Her cousin, Mary, was the
queen of Scotland.
She thought she should be
queen of England, too.

Mary Stuart, Queen of Scotland, lost her throne in 1567.

S. PAULES CHURCH.

THAMESIS

An old engraving showing the Thames River, St. Paul's Cathedral, and the Globe Theater where the plays of Shakespeare were performed.

Then Mary lost her throne.
She came to England
to ask Elizabeth for help.

Elizabeth couldn't trust her.
Mary was too dangerous.
So Elizabeth made her stay
in a castle in the north.

Chapter 4

Friends and Enemies

Elizabeth knew that a queen
cannot trust everybody.
Some people will do anything
just to get more power.

Once, some men tried to put
William Cecil in prison.
Elizabeth stopped them.
Cecil was her friend.
She *could* trust him.

Then people began to fight
about religion again.
Some wanted to free Mary,
make her queen,
and change England's religion.

Lord Hunsdon

Elizabeth's cousin,
Hunsdon, stopped them.
She could trust him, too.

Thomas Howard, the
Duke of Norfolk

But another cousin,
Norfolk, wanted
Mary to be queen.
He helped with a plan
to kill Elizabeth.

That plan failed
and Elizabeth had
Norfolk's head cut off.

In 1587 Queen Elizabeth (right) signed the death warrant of Mary, Queen of Scots (below).

But Mary didn't give up.
She helped with a new plan.
As last, Elizabeth had
Mary's head cut off, too.
She hated doing that.
But she couldn't trust Mary.

Elizabeth did trust
her sailors.
They made her
feel good. Some
found new ways
to India and China.
Trading companies
were started
and England
grew richer.

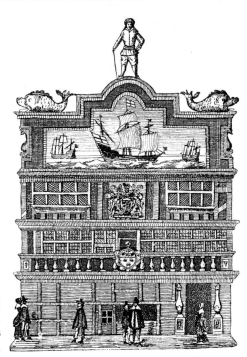

The ships (above), seal (center), and
office (right) of the East India Company.
The trade routes established by this
company brought new wealth to England.

Queen Elizabeth knighting Francis Drake

Sir Francis Drake

Francis Drake sailed
all around the world.
One day, Elizabeth stood
on the deck of his ship
and made him a knight.

The story is told that Sir Walter Raleigh (right) once spread his cloak over a mud puddle so Queen Elizabeth would not get her shoes dirty.

Walter Raleigh started
colonies in America.
He named Virginia for Elizabeth,
who was known as "The Virgin Queen."
He wrote poems about her, too.

Elizabeth would need
all her brave sailors,
because soon England
would be at war with Spain.

King Philip the Second of Spain sent his armada, a fleet
of 130 armed ships, to invade England in 1588.

Chapter 5

Her Greatest Jewel

Elizabeth hated war.
She felt that peace
was better for her people.

But a huge fleet of Spanish
ships called the
Spanish Armada sailed
into the English Channel.
England had to fight.

Queen Elizabeth spoke
to her soldiers
and sailors before
the big battle at sea.
her words stirred
the hearts of all
who heard her.

Elizabeth made a speech
to cheer on her troops.

"Let tyrants fear," she said.
"... Under God, I have placed
my strength and good will
in the loyal hearts and
good will of my subjects."

She said her body was weak,
"but I have the heart
... of a king."

The smaller, faster English ships were able to turn back the bigger Spanish ships.

**All England cheered Queen Elizabeth
and rejoiced at the defeat of the Spanish Armada.**

In almost no time,
her loyal subjects smashed
the Spanish Armada to pieces.
Once again, England was safe.

Queen Elizabeth at prayer

As Elizabeth grew older,
her friends began to die.
When Robert Dudley died,
she locked herself in her room.
Some people say he was
the only man she ever loved.

William Cecil died, too.
He left his son, Robert,
to take his place.
But Elizabeth missed Cecil.

Still, she had good times.
Music filled her court.
People gave her fine gifts.
She saw beautiful plays
by William Shakespeare.

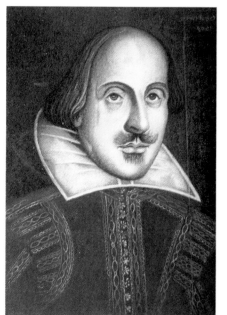

Queen Elizabeth liked good music (opposite page) and literature. The queen and her court read the poetry and watched the plays written by William Shakespeare (left).

When Queen Elizabeth traveled,
the members of her court
went with her. She was
always surrounded by people.

Elizabeth liked to visit
different parts of England.
People cheered as she rode by.
They held big parties
and gave her more gifts.

For a while,
a man called Essex
seemed to be part
of the good times.
He made Elizabeth feel
young and happy again.

**The Earl of Essex,
Robert Devereux,
was convicted of
treason and executed.**

But then he tried
to get rid of her
and make himself king.
Elizabeth had to
have him killed, too.

Elizabeth had many jewels.
She even had a ruby
as big as a tennis ball.
But in her last speech
she said her greatest jewel
was the love of her people.

Queen Elizabeth the First
of England died in 1603.
Because she did so much for
England while she was queen,
the years she ruled are called the
Golden Age or the Elizabethan Age.

Elizabeth the First died
when she was 69.
The baby girl that
no one wanted
had turned out to be
one of England's greatest rulers.

Important Dates

1533   September 7—Born at Greenwich Palace, England, to Henry Tudor (Henry the Eighth) and Anne Boleyn

1554   Sent to Tower of London by Queen Mary

1558   Proclaimed queen of England

1562   Caught smallpox

1569   Northern Rebellion put down

1587   Mary, Queen of Scots, executed

1588   Spanish Armada defeated

1601   Essex Rebellion put down

1603   March 24—Died at Richmond Palace, England

INDEX

Page numbers in boldface type indicate illustrations.

PHOTO CREDITS

ABOUT THE AUTHOR

Carol Greene has degrees in English Literature and Musicology. She has worked in international exchange programs, as an editor, and as a teacher. She now lives in St. Louis, Missouri, and writes full-time. She has published more than eighty books. Others in the Rookie Biographies series include *Benjamin Franklin, Pocahontas, Martin Luther King, Jr., Christopher Columbus, Abraham Lincoln, Robert E. Lee, Ludwig van Beethoven, Laura Ingalls Wilder, Jackie Robinson, Jacques Cousteau, Daniel Boone, Louis Pasteur,* and *Chief Joseph.*